The Monster Under the Bed

by Cameron Macintosh

illustrated by Volker Beisler

OXFORD

UNIVERSITY PRESS

AUSTRALIA & NEW ZEALAND

Chapter 1
A strange noise

After a busy day of school, sport and reading, Mark was enjoying a very deep sleep. He was dreaming about swimming in a pool of jelly when a strange burping noise woke him.

Mark sat up. The noise seemed to be coming from under his bed.

'This has to be a dream,' he thought. 'There's nothing under my bed that could make a burping noise!'

Mark soon went back to sleep. A few hours later, another strange burping sound woke him again. This time, he knew he hadn't been dreaming. He climbed out of bed, grabbed his torch and pointed it under his bed.

Mark jumped backwards. Hiding under the bed was a fluffy pink monster.

As Mark looked the monster in the eye, he could see it shaking. 'It seems to be more worried about me than I am about it,' he thought.

"I'm not going to hurt you," he said to the monster.

The monster stopped shaking and started making a burping noise again.

"Would you like something to eat?" asked Mark.

The monster's eyes opened wide.

"Stay there," said Mark. "I'll be back in a minute."

He rushed to the kitchen.

Mark went back to his room with some crackers. He put one on the floor, just in front of his bed. A fluffy pink arm slid out from under the bed, grabbed the cracker and dragged it back under.

Mark put another cracker down and this time three arms slid out. He put a cracker on each of them. The arms slid back under the bed and soon Mark could hear a happy munching sound.

Then, Mark heard a snore. He looked under the bed and saw that the monster was fast asleep.

Mark climbed back into bed. It took him ages to go back to sleep!

Chapter 2
A new friend

The next morning, Mark wondered if his meeting with the monster had been a dream. He looked over the side of his bed and saw crumbs on the floor. Just then, a long pink arm slid out.

"Sorry," said Mark, "I don't have any more crackers. I'll bring some back after breakfast."

When Mark sat down to have breakfast with his parents, he ate as quickly as he could. On his way out of the kitchen, he grabbed another five crackers.

When Mark went back to his room, the monster ate the crackers right away.

"I have to go to school today," Mark said to the monster. "Here are some books you can read while I'm gone." Mark slid the books under the bed and got ready for school.

All day, Mark found it hard to think about anything but the monster under his bed. He knew that he couldn't tell anyone about it. He thought that if his parents found the monster they might send it to the zoo.

When Mark got home, he rushed straight to his room. The monster was reading one of his books. Mark slid under the bed beside the monster.

"I don't know what you are, or how you got here, but I think you need a name," he said. "How about Pinky?"

Pinky nodded and gave Mark a high five with one of its eight arms.

Then, they both read Mark's books together and had lots of laughs.

Soon, Mark could hear Pinky's tummy making strange noises again.

"I'll get you some crackers," he said.

Chapter 3
Feed the monster

Over the next few days, Mark kept feeding Pinky the family's crackers.

   At the end of the week, Mum said, "You've been eating way too many crackers, Mark. I'd like you to snack on fruit from now on."

After dinner that night, Mark took some fruit and cheese to Pinky. The moment he slid them under the bed, they flew back out.

"What's wrong?" asked Mark. "Don't you like fruit or cheese?" Pinky made an even louder burping noise.

"I see," said Mark. "I'll find you something else."

As his parents watched television that evening, Mark made some toast and jam. He ran back to his room and gave it to Pinky. This time, he heard loud munching sounds under the bed and he knew that Pinky was happy.

Chapter 4
A new home?

Over the next week, Mark saw that Pinky was growing and was taking up most of the space beneath the bed. Soon, Mark's bed was lifting off the floor and wobbling strangely. It was getting very hard to sleep in!

'I like Pinky a lot,' thought Mark, 'but I'm going to have to find him a new home.'

The next morning, Mark looked in every corner of the house for somewhere safe for Pinky to live. There was nowhere inside the house, so he looked in the garden. There was a shed, but it was full of garden tools.

As Mark went back to the house, he saw a big empty area under the deck. It was just the right size!

That night, after Mum and Dad went to bed, Mark found some old pillows and made a nice warm bed under the deck. Then, he made lots of jam toast and made a trail of it, all the way from the bed to the back door. Pinky came out from under the bed and ate every slice.

Mark opened the door. With the last slice of toast, he led Pinky down the steps and under the deck.

"There you go, Pinky," he said. "A nice warm place, all for you! You will not feel so squashed here!"

Slowly, Pinky crawled in and curled up on the pillows. Mark wished him a good night and crept back inside.

Pinky was very happy in his new home. Mark was happy too, knowing that Pinky was safe. Each day he brought snacks to Pinky and lots of books to read, too!